About POLPERRO

Michael Williams

BOSSINEY BOOKS

Books consulted:

The History of Polperro, Jonathan Couch, Dyllansow Truran, 1986; Around & About The Smugglers' Ways, Bossiney, 1991; The Rooks of Trelawne, Andrew Lanyon, The Photographers Gallery 1976; East Cornwall in the Old Days, Joy Wilson, Bossiney 1988; Portrait of Polperro, Sheila de Burlet, Bantam 1977.

The author wishes to thank Peter and Bridget Bishop of The Pottery Shop, Polperro for commissioning this publication and for all their help and encouragement. He is especially indebted to Dick Jolliff for a fascinating interview and for reading the contents. Thanks also go to the Cornish Studies Library at Redruth, Robert Hicks MP for assistance in obtaining information concerning the 1976 floods, Anthea Barker for help in research, Angela Larcombe for her editing, and last but not least Felicity Young and Ray Bishop for their especially commissioned drawings and photographs.

ACKNOWLEDGEMENTS:
Front cover photography: Roy Westlake
Front cover design: Maggie Ginger
Back cover photography: Ray Bishop
Modern photography: Ray Bishop; AG Bartlett
Drawings: Felicity Young

© Michael Williams

Published by Bossiney Books, St Teath, Bodmin, Cornwall.
Typeset and printed by Penwell Print, Callington, Cornwall.

ISBN 0 948158 76 X

About The Author . . .

MICHAEL WILLIAMS, a Cornishman, started full-time publishing in 1975. He and his wife Sonia live in a cottage on the shoulder of a green valley just outside St Teath in North Cornwall.

In addition to publishing and writing Michael Williams is a keen cricketer and collector of cricket books and autographs. He was the first captain of the Cornish Crusaders Cricket Club and is today President of the Crusaders. He is also a member of Cornwall and Gloucestershire County Cricket Clubs. A member of the RSPCA and the International League for the Protection of Horses, he has worked hard for reform in laws relating to animal welfare. In 1984 he was elected to The Ghost Club.

His latest Cornish contribution to the Bossiney list was Supernatural Search in Cornwall. *He is currently working on* Curious Cornwall. *Here, in words and pictures, he explores Polperro.*

Polperro?

SOME historians think the village's name derived from Peter's Pool. In its time Polperro has acquired many titles. Bishop Brantyngham's Register, in 1396, referred to Porthpyre; a deed belonging to the reign of Henry V used the word Poppere; a chart in the British Museum bears the name Polpyz – interpreted as meaning fish pool – ; Holinshed used the word Polpir; and Leland, in his writings, gave it as many as three. Less affectionately, the port has been known – because of the smell of offal – as Polstink! But today there's no dispute: Polperro is Polperro.

Who can run down from its great heights into its great depths and forget it?

Arthur Mee called it 'the Clovelly of Cornwall', but there is an important difference: no car can go to Clovelly, and no car does. But authorised cars are permitted in Polperro. However, there are stringent restrictions for visitors – use the car parks is the only advice. Without them, there would be chaos.

When Mrs Bray, the Tavistock writer, came here in the 1830s there were no cars of course, but the following word picture from the lady shows access to Polperro was no easy matter in those days either: '*Looe,*' says she, '*beautiful as it is, is not to be compared to Polperro, two miles distant from Trelawne. The descent to it is so steep, that I, who was not accustomed to the path, could only get down by clinging to Mr Bray's arm for support; it was slippery, and so rocky that in some places there were steps cut in the road for the convenience of the passenger. The view of the little port, the old town in the bottom (if town it can be called), the cliffs, and the spiked rocks, that start up in the wildest and most abrupt manner, breaking the direct sweep of the waves towards the harbour, altogether produced such a combination of magnificent coast scenery as may truly be called sublime.*'

Polperro is often a very busy resort in the summer season. Tourism has become the golden goose. So if you can select your time in the calendar, come here in the off-season when something of the old magic remains. Polperro is a classic example of how such places needed – back in 1920 or thereabouts – the imposing of strict controls in relation to buildings, advertising, electrification etc. Around then tourism and 'progress' began to dominate.

Alongside and above the church, steps climb high above the village.

A painter busy at his easel in the Polperro harbour of old.

With sensible restrictions imposed, Polperro would have retained an even greater percentage of its old world charm. As it is, the village, with its picturesque qualities and deep sense of history, remains one of the gems of not only Cornwall – but the whole of the Westcountry – and the thousands of visitors who keep returning are testimony to that fact.

The huge south coast cliffs help to protect the village from the worst conditions of the Channel. Nevertheless it has been necessary to provide bulwarks to keep the inner harbour and Polperro itself safe from the wildest of winter storms. The eastern cliffs, known as The Warren, offer some attractive coastline walks – and there are superlative sea vistas.

It is no surprise that Polperro and its surrounding coastline have drawn so many painters like a magnet. The attractions are subtle and various: deeper than the sea and the cliffs, the harbour and the boats, the narrow streets and the old cottages. The varying light, the changing mood, the ancient traditions all play their part. The painting tradition goes on today. An art gallery is based in the 19th century ex-Ebenezer Chapel, where the East Cornwall Society of Artists stage their exhibitions.

Before the explosion of tourism Polperro must have been one of the most picturesque spots on the south coast of Cornwall. '. . . *a small and quaint*

A bird's eye view of Polperro.

fishing village lying in a hollow between two rocky hills . . .' was how *The Directory of Cornwall* described it in 1914.

Thirty years ago Sir John Betjeman, a man who knew and loved his Cornwall, came here and reflected: '*I can remember Polperro when it smelt of fresh fish instead of fried and had one antique shop, a secondhand bookshop, a few artists' studios and fishing was still the chief industry. The houses were of grey slate with white painted glazing bars to the windows. The mesembryanthemum in early summer made a mauve and green contrast with the old grey cottages below*'.

The cottages of Polperro cluster tightly together – and neighbours lived cheek by jowl. This small boy may now be an elderly gentleman who can remember the tales of smuggling told him by his grandfather.

Smuggling

POLPERRO and smuggling went together naturally – like strawberries and Cornish cream.

The harbour and the closeness to the French coast were not the only factors. Polperro, with its labyrinth of winding, narrow streets, its maze of cottages and cellars was ideal for illegal goings-on. The cramped shape of the place made it perfect for the smugglers: nipping in or out of cottages and into another street in a matter of seconds. The closeness of the cottages, enabling families to tap warnings on the walls to one another, all helped to shape and sustain the illicit traffic.

Another reason for the flourishing free trade was the skill of the local boatbuilders who turned out swift-moving craft, clippers which 'could scud away from the fastest of the Government cruisers, and offer them a tow-line in derision.' One Polperro vessel, *The Unity*, made as many as 500 excursions. The co-operation of local people made it a first-class rendezvous for the smugglers; a headache for the authorities. One of the first resident Excise units was based at Polperro, but it was badly received. Nobody would accommodate the Excisemen in the village and they were forced to live on a boat in the harbour.

Smuggling in the 18th and 19th centuries may make good reading for us today and, of course, all layers of Cornish society were involved; the gentry bought their wine and spirits at 'cut' prices and, on occasion, Customs House men connived. But there was a dark, wicked side to much of the smuggler's work: deeds stained with murder and corruption, treachery and violence.

Fellow Bossiney author David Mudd in his admirable *Around & About The Smugglers' Ways* recalled the seedy society involved:

'In the great and colourful days of smuggling, Cornwall's pubs held a colourful collection of some of the less attractive members of society. There would be the smuggler and some of his crew; the merchant who would buy or arrange shipments; the informer who might tell the smugglers of some forthcoming Customs or Coastguard operation; or the undercover agent

The harbour and the closeness of the French coast played a big part in Polperro's smuggling history.

listening to every fragment of conversation in the hope it would lead to an arrest and a seizure of contraband.

'There would be the stool-pigeon willing to assist either side against each other; and customers who were delighted to buy cut-price spirits, tobacco, tea or coffee.'

One Polperro man, Roger Toms gave evidence in court against a smuggler guilty of murder and, as a result, dared not show his face in the village again. It's reputed the rhyme: 'Tell tale tit, your tongue shall be slit' originated here. Everybody, including his family, turned against Toms. He appealed to the authorities for protection, and, in their wisdom, they gave him a dreary job in prison service. Many years later he died at Newgate in protective custody.

It was a strange world. For instance, the man who ran the business side of smuggling hereabouts was Zephaniah Job, who hailed from St Agnes on the north coast. It was Job who organized the loading and the unloading, the hiring of horses from the local farms, the careful planning of being in the right place at the right time and clearing the cargoes before night turned into daylight. The respectable side to Mr Job was his role as banker and business manager for the gentry, including the Trelawneys of Trelawne. Often Sir Harry Trelawney borrowed money from Job and his smuggling colleagues, but nobody would accept an IOU, bearing the baronet's signature unless it was countersigned by Job – despite Sir Harry being a Justice of the Peace and an ordained clergyman. Strange world indeed.

Zephaniah Job was, in fact, a considerable all-rounder. He was largely responsible for the pilchard trade between Polperro and Italy. He was a coal importer, a seed merchant and a corn trader, and leased the local lime kilns. He worked everyday except Sundays and Christmas Day. A meticulous man with figures, he kept accounts for several vessels which were used as privateers – these were privately owned, licensed by the Admiralty to attack and, when possible, capture enemy ships. His principal clients were the Rowetts and the Quillers – who made outstanding contributions to British war efforts in the period 1777 to 1815. Mr Job even issued his own Polperro bank notes. Truly a colourful character who might have belonged to Cornish fiction rather than genuine history.

The smugglers however did not rate themselves as members of the criminal class – far from it. They saw themselves as 'fair traders' who, in the

Bossiney author Felicity Young walks down a Polperro street in winter. Smugglers enjoyed the advantages of easy communication from cottage to cottage.

words of Adam Smith's historic definition, '*were incapable of violating the laws of natural justice, and who would have been in every respect excellent citizens had not the laws of the country made that a crime which Nature had never meant to be so.*'

There is no doubt the deep poverty of Cornish fishermen and miners was greatly alleviated by cash and goods from the smuggling trade. So much so that one aged Cornish woman, with a sharp memory, told Sabine Baring-Gould: '*Oh, dear! oh, dear what is the world coming to – for education and all kinds o'wickedness? Sure, there's no smuggling now, and poor folks ha'n't got the means o'bettering themselves like proper Christians.*'

That splendid Westcountry character parson and writer Robert Stephen Hawker has given us a diamond-sharp insight into the smuggling operation:

A half-hidden moon, muffled oars and a rocky cove – Felicity Young draws on her imagination to create a scene from the days of smuggling.

'The rough sea-captain, half smuggler, half pirate, who ran his lugger by beacon-light into some rugged cove among the massive headlands of the shore, and was relieved of his freight by the active and diligent "countryside." This was the term allotted to that chosen troop of native sympathisers who were always ready to rescue and conceal the stores that had escaped the degradation of the gauger's brand. Men yet alive relate with glee how they used to rush at some well-known signal to the strand, their small active horses shaved from forelock to tail, smoother than any modern clip, well soaped or greased from head to foot, so as to slip easily out of any hostile grasp; and then with a double keg or pack slung on to every nag by a single girth, away went the whole herd led by some swift well trained mare, to the inland cave or rocky hold, the shelter of their spoil.'

The smugglers had the wit and foresight to advise local people when their contingent travelled through their village or hamlet, they should face the wall. Consequently if smugglers were arrested the villagers could, with hands on heart, say they had *seen nothing*.

'*Them that ask no questions isn't told a lie, watch the wall, my darling, while the gentlemen go by.*'

Dr Jonathan Couch

IT IS interesting how now and then a character somehow personifies his or her area. One thinks of Sir Arthur Quiller-Couch and Fowey, Robert Stephen Hawker and Morwenstow, Sabine Baring-Gould and Lewtrenchard. Here at Polperro it is Dr Jonathan Couch. Like Sir Humphry Davy, he was a gifted versatile Cornishman, a man who made a considerable contribution to scientific knowledge.

Couch's early education was rooted firmly in this part of Cornwall: first at a Dame's School in the village, moving on to a boarding school at Lansallos and later to the Grammar School at Bodmin – all of which paved the way for medical studies in London. There he was deeply influenced by some of the leading medical men of the day. He came back to his home village in 1810 to begin a lifelong service to the community. It was a brave and loyally Cornish decision, for he had given up the prospect of becoming a successful and well-paid London surgeon to become a relatively poorly

Couch's House and Saxon Bridge photographed earlier this century.

paid Cornish doctor – but it was a decision which enabled him to pursue his natural history studies.

As a doctor Couch was ahead of his time. For example when there was an outbreak of smallpox in Polperro in 1837, he vaccinated and inoculated more than 400 patients – this at a time when there was doubt, even downright opposition to vaccination against smallpox. But the people of Polperro trusted their doctor. Through the years he must have walked or ridden hundreds of miles visiting his patients. The narrow lanes in and out of the village were too steep for a horse-drawn carriage and, on occasion, he struggled through snowdrifts to reach people in need.

But his life was not all medicine. Jonathan Couch was a natural historian who would rush down to the quayside to paint meticulous watercolour sketches of fish – fish which had been brought ashore in pails of sea water so that the Doctor could see them in their natural glory. At other times local men and boys would bring lobsters, seaweed, crabs and jellyfish to his house in Lansallos Street. He wrote and illustrated what was for years the standard work on British fishes. In the words of Andrew Lanyon: 'Couch became a kind of seaside Gilbert White.'

'The Old Doctor', who remembered seeing Tennyson strolling through the village carrying the very first umbrella he had seen, loved recording local legends and history. His *History of Polperro*, first published in 1871, was a classic of its kind.

He married three times. His first wife Jane died in childbirth, and his second wife was another Jane – daughter of Richard Quiller – and when her mother died, they moved into the Quiller family home which became known as Couch's House – a name it bears to this day. They had six children, and three of their sons became doctors. At the age of 70, the Doctor surprised Polperro and the surrounding countryside by marrying Sarah Lander Roose who was only 22.

In 1879, Jonathan died peacefully in his sleep at his home by the little bridge over the stream. His grandson was Sir Arthur Quiller-Couch of Fowey who, until the arrival of Dr A.L. Rowse, was the best-known Cornish writer. 'Q' made Couch's House the residence of his hero in his novel *Nicky-Nan, Reservist*. The 'Polpier' of that piece of fiction is based on the real Polperro which 'Q' remembered early in this century.

Couch's House photographed by Ray Bishop in the autumn of 1991.

*Dick Jolliff in his natural element
– aboard a boat in the harbour.*

A Fisherman's Memories

IN DR Couch's day, as many as two-thirds of the Polperro population was engaged in 'fishing and other maritime pursuits.'
In those times the pilchard was the mainstay of the industry.
Generations of Polperro men followed a family tradition of going to sea as fishermen. One man, who personifies that Polperro tradition, is Dick Jolliff who was born and bred in the village. Dick, now in his mid-70s, has diamond-sharp memories of earlier days. 'My father was a fisherman, my grandfather too, and my mother's father too. She was a Mark, descended from the local smuggler who was shot and lies buried in Talland Churchyard.'
We talked at his cottage in Lansallos Street one Saturday afternoon in winter: 'Back in the 1920s and 1930s I can remember as many as 100 fishermen in Polperro . . . forty boats driving for pilchards and there were smaller boats. Then the pilchard was our most important fish, and we had three pilchard factories in the village. Two of the factories were owned by Italians. The pilchards were left in the brine for three weeks, and they tested

the strength of the brine by placing a potato in it to see if it would float. If it did, the brine was correct. After the oil had been pressed out of the pilchards they were then shipped to Genoa, Italy.'

There was good reason then for the Cornish toast that went:

'Here's health to the Pope, may he live to repent
And add half the year to the time of his Lent,
To teach all his children from Rome to the Poles
There's nothing like pilchards for saving their souls.'

But Dick says 'When Mussolini invaded Abyssinia, sanctions were introduced against Italy and that virtually killed the pilchard trade. Though it was revived, after the war the fish were tinned. In the pre-war days it was big business; you'd get a local farmer who might take a thousand fish and salt them in cloam jars.

'In the old days most of the fishermen were strict Methodists and we never went to sea on a Sunday. It was a good life but a hard one. Sometimes you'd be kept in the harbour for as long as ten to twelve weeks through

Fisherman Dick Jolliff in earlier days.

Polperro   Cornwall

Polperro in the days when the pilchard was the mainstay of the fishing industry.

rough weather, and when you went to sea you'd perhaps land a good catch and you might make £75 from that catch, and that money would be shared by four hands. Then you had the expense of the boat. So there was no fortune to be made from fishing.'

A modest man, Dick declined to talk about the dangers – and the bravery – of fishing folk. But we have Dr Couch's word on the subject: '. . . a hardy race of men, often leading a life of no little peril . . . their gains are rarely considerable and at all times precarious.'

In the words of Dick Jolliff: 'The worst winds we had to encounter would be the north winds which on many occasions would be a south westerly and then very suddenly with a squall of rain would fly to the north. Often it would be one man to the pump until we got to harbour. We closed the harbour in bad weather with heavy baulks of timber . . . a very dangerous job when a gale was blowing in the harbour and when it was dark as we had only a hand winch at that time.

'The fishing divided itself into two seasons June, July and August was the

Polperro Harbour in 1992 – a contrast from the days when there were ▶ as many as 100 fishermen in Polperro.

18

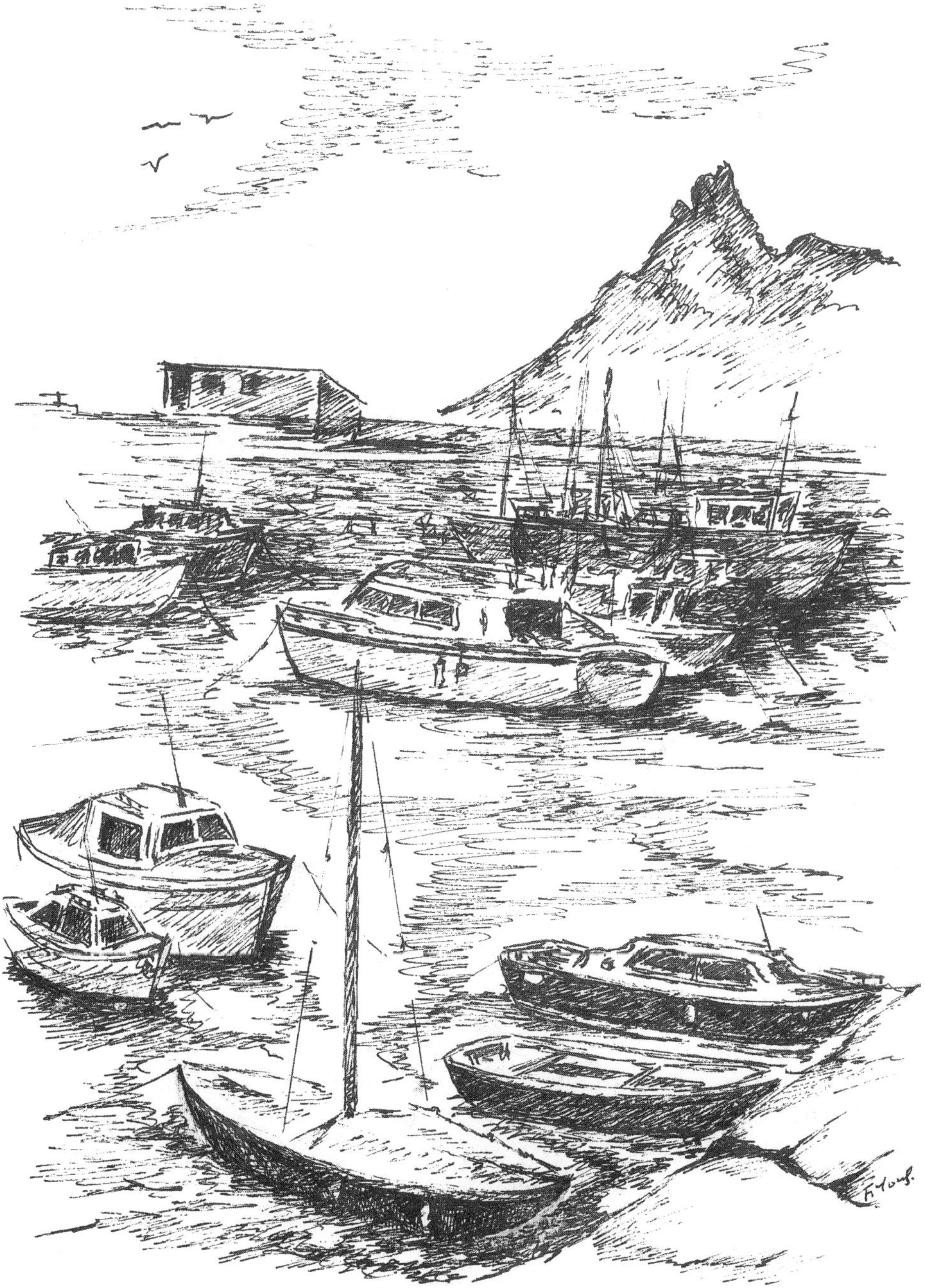

A postcard from Polperro in 1932 – the sender tells of exploring the cottages and cliffs by moonlight and calls the little fishing port 'enchantingly beautiful'.

Below, a cluster of fishermen's houses and stores, a working area with just one curious onlooker standing on the harbour side.

summer season, and then we had another season in November, December and January. After that the fish were spent; they'd get thin with nothing much on them. We fished over quite a wide area, from Start Point down to the Lizard.

'There were four large coppers known as a "furnace" for barking the nets. This had to be carried out every six weeks during the pilchard season and when the season was over the nets would be run through creosote and be dried and then be put into the net lofts.

'The last pier to be built at Polperro was The Duke of Cornwall Pier, the breakwater on the eastern side of the outer harbour, known as the "hauen". The foundation stone was laid on September 5 1861 and it was completed on January 1 1862, costing £627.

'The level ground by the first seat on Chaypel Cliffs was known as Chaypel Stanin Place because the people of Polperro stood there dressed in red pretending to be soldiers when the Spanish Armada sailed up the English Channel.'

As a boy he can vividly remember the click of his mother's knitting needles. 'Mother made hundreds of Cornish Guernseys and sold them at half a crown a time.' A lifelong Methodist and teetotaller, Dick Jolliff has been a lay preacher for more than fifty years, and still preaches the occasional sermon. Recently when a religious television programme was made at Polperro, he took part. 'There were close links between Methodism and Liberalism among the fishermen. In my lifetime I can recall several Polperro fishermen as local preachers, and, for a time, we had Mr Isaac Foot as our MP, a great Liberal and Methodist.

'In the Methodist chapel every year we held the Harvest of the Sea service, when the chapel would be decorated with nets, crab pots, and other fishing tackle, and the Polperro Fishermen's Choir would sing Sankey hymns connected with the sea.'

He is proud too of John's Wesley's links with the village. 'Wesley on his horse would have come down Talland Hill to Polperro. For a thousand years that was the way you came into the village. It wasn't until July 1849 that the New Road was opened, and they got most of the money for that from public subscription.

'When I was a boy Polperro was almost all Polperro people, and fishing dominated village life. From the last cottage in the Warren into the Harbour

The actress Rita Tushingham, photographed in her former home high above Polperro.

bridge, there lived forty fishermen – that's fathers and sons – now, by contrast, there is only one working fisherman living there, and two retired fishermen.

'Properties have changed too. Once you could buy a cottage for a few hundred pounds! And, of course, more and more houses have been built in the village, and the character of the place has changed . . . more and more upcountry people have bought holiday cottages.' But you get the definite impression he would not have wanted to live anywhere else.

Paul Eddington, the television and theatre actor, was brought up in Polperro, and Dick recalls others who had links with the village. 'Hugh Walpole, Angela Brazil, who wrote children's books, Walter Greenwood, who made the film 'Love on the Dole', Freddie Cook, the artist, Cecil Williamson, of the smuggling museum, Roland Emmett, the cartoonist for *Punch*, and yes the actress Rita Tushingham . . . they all had their time in Polperro.'

His fund of local knowledge is enormous. I asked him, for example, about

The Jews House – a name without any apparent foundation.

some of the strange Polperro house names, places like the Old Jews House. Dick chuckled: 'We had this character here who went around putting fancy names on houses to add a little local colour. You're right, there were not many Jews in Cornwall . . . they found the Cornish tough opposition!'

His memories include the local bakehouse which 'was heated with faggots of wood, brought from Trelawne Woods by horse and wagon. Faggots placed in the brick oven were lit and when the heat was considered sufficient the fine wood ash was raked out. The dinners were put in on a long handled shovel. In the afternoons saffron cake, pasties and bread would be put in. A favourite dish was potted fish which would be pilchards, mackerel or conger; the fish would be put into a cloam jar then sprinkled with pepper and salt, a little cochineal for colouring, then vinegar and bay leaves would be added and a sheet of brown paper tied over the top with the person's name on it. This would be taken along in the afternoon when everything else had been cooked, put into the oven and left simmering overnight. Pilchards were also cooked on the grid iron. The fish were cleaned and a little salt rubbed into the belly . . . then cooked over an open fire. If a girl from the country married a fisherman Polperro people had a saying "What do her know about scrowing a pilchard on a grid iron." '

The Cornish

TODAY Cornwall and places like Polperro in particular, are a combination of natives and people from upalong, from the other side of the Tamar. Time was, before the birth of tourism, when Cornwall was almost entirely peopled by the Cornish.

The Cornishman – and the Cornish woman – was, at heart, Non-Conformist. In religion and in politics, Cornwall has often gone against the tide. It is no mere accident the Cornish language is still alive and Cornish Nationalism stirs in hearts and minds.

The old Cornish were like their landscape, an ancient knowing race, withdrawn to strangers, existing as much in the past as in the here and now.

The biographer R. Glyn Grylls, writing in the long extinct *Cornish Review*, had this to say:

'*The thing about the Cornish is that they are not nice: exciting and attrac-*

Sam Puckey, a fisherman, decorated his Polperro home with shells from all over the world. Today, Sam's old house is known as the Shell House.

tive but not nice. They have colour enough to turn the spectacles of most onlookers pink but it is not fast to light. The impulsiveness that goes as far as magnanimity does not sustain generosity; the devotion, loyal to fanaticism, has no fidelity; the forthcomingness keeps much more back than reticence – like an iceberg two-thirds under the water, if there were not anything less like an iceberg than any Celt . . . Where does it go, then, all the colour? The warm tones of manner, the light and shade of speech? The colour goes into the personality. Almost one might say it is enough for the Cornish to be Cornish; but not quite for they have a full measure of Celtic discontent. The energy that makes for colourfulness goes into the business of living – always a hard one in Cornwall – the fervour into congregational worship, into a personal relationship with omnipotence, not into embellishing its dwelling-place; the enterprise into seeking fortunes afield.'

John Wesley

JOHN Wesley hit Cornwall and the Cornish like a gale of wind. Religion of a kind is bred into the bone of the Cornish. Emotional and instinctive, many of them reacted immediately to the preacher on horseback.

Wesley's physical achievements alone were enormous. He rode more than 250,000 miles, on occasions covering 70 miles and preaching three sermons in the same day. Throughout his lifetime he preached more than 45,000 sermons. He had 233 original works published, earned £40,000 from his writing, and gave every penny of it away. In addition to all this, he set up a free medical dispensary, adapted an electrical machine for healing, opened spinning and knitting shops for the poor, and founded the Kingswood School for boys at Bristol, writing the text books himself.

The great preacher made two visits to Polperro. Of his first visit he wrote in his *Journal*: '*1762, Wednesday September 1st. I came about two to Polperro, a little village, four hours ride from Plymouth passage, surrounded with high mountains. However, abundance of people had found their way thither. And so had Satan too; for an old grey-headed sinner was busily cursing all the Methodists just as we came into town. However, God gave his blessing, both to us and the congregation.*'

Robert Jeffrey

SOME slices of Cornish history read like fiction. Robert Jeffrey, the son of a Polperro inn keeper, is one such case. Jeffrey is a man who is remembered for something that happened to him rather than anything he achieved. He was impressed into the Navy at the age of 18, and he had the misfortune to find himself serving under a cruel captain when he made the mistake of stealing some rum – and getting found out! Captain Lake's punishment was to leave the unfortunate Cornishman on an uninhabited island in mid-ocean.

The islet of Sombrero, one of the Leeward group, was 'desolate and treeless, a naked lump of rock, with no springs. Jeffrey suffered frightfully from hunger, and worse from thirst.' It was eight days before Jeffrey was spotted and rescued by a passing ship. During those eight days and nights Jeffrey must have wondered whether he would ever see Polperro again. Anyway he

Bridges are a notable feature in many of our Cornish villages and here Felicity Young has captured the sturdy beauty of a small bridge in Polperro.

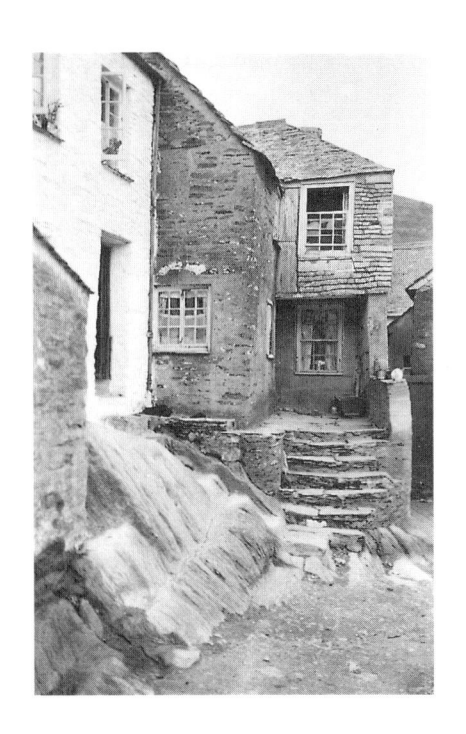

A corner of Polperro showing the typical village steps. A white cat perches on a convenient wall.

The Smugglers' Cave, Polperro. Local caves, according to Britain's top ghost hunter Peter Underwood, are haunted by two restless spirits. In his Ghosts of Cornwall *Mr Underwood tells the tale of two smugglers who fell out over the division of some gold. In the fight one died and is reputed to haunt the caves still looking for his share of the gold. The other Polperro phantom is believed to be that of Willy Willock, a fisherman who decided to explore the subterranean labyrinth – and was never seen again.*

eventually found himself in America where he worked as a blacksmith – completely oblivious of the fact that his 'punishment' was being debated in the House of Commons.

Captain Lake was duly court martialled, and Jeffrey eventually found.

On Robert Jeffrey's return to his home village of Polperro there was great rejoicing. Though he had not bothered to write to his mother, the whole village turned out to meet him with flags flying and the band playing. The young Cornishman's career now took a curious turn. He hired himself out to some of the minor London theatres to be exhibited as 'Jeffrey the Sailor'. After a few months, he returned to Cornwall with enough money to buy a small schooner for the coasting trade, but it was an ill-fated piece of speculation. Jeffrey 'fell into consumption' and died leaving a wife and daughter in deep poverty. He was just 31.

The 1976 Storm

FRIDAY, September 24 1976 is a date Polperro will never forget. That evening at about 8pm a thunderstorm broke over the village and within 15 minutes water was cascading through the streets in terrifying fashion, damaging more than 100 properties.

Next day in the *Western Evening Herald* journalist Michael Taylor wrote: *'The cost of the floodwater wall of death that thundered through an unsuspecting Polperro last night will never be measured. A life has been lost – 81 year-old Mr William Haycock was swept away – people injured, others thrust into deep shock by the tragedy of it all, and properties and cars have been ruined by the merciless wave of water.*

'The quiet, unassuming villagers of Polperro will never be the same . . . the narrow streets resembled a disaster area. The storm, and what it brought, has left Polperro a mini Lynmouth.'

Mr Sellick Giles, then aged 70, a resident of Talland Hill, said 'The whole centre was under several feet of water, and the trickle of the stream – the river Pol – was a gushing torrent that completely covered the stone bridge called Saxon Bridge.'

The resolve of Polperro and its people to put this terrible Black Friday behind it was personified by one elderly resident Jenny Hanson, 79 at the

Local people retrieve cars washed into the river by the floodwater at Crumplehorn Mill.

time, who lived at the Big Green House in Fore Street, and 'read' tea cups – she had done a reading for the actress Rita Tushingham. Speaking to the *Western Morning News*, Mrs Hanson said, 'I knew it was going to rain, but not like this!'

A *Sunday Telegraph* reporter sent these words back to his newspaper in London: *'The picture postcard Cornish seaside village of Polperro was a scene of "utter devastation" yesterday after being hit by floods caused by thunder storms and high tides.*

'Scores of families took refuge in upstairs rooms as houses were flooded to a depth of seven feet. Parked cars were "picked up like toys" and flung into the river.'

How did such flooding occur?

There was a combination of factors. First, the local geography, with the valley becoming a narrow funnel, through which too much water tried to pass in too short a time. Then there was the deep depression which came off the Atlantic Ocean, laden with water it had picked up from the sub-tropics around Bermuda. Thirdly there was a freakish element. Elsewhere in East Cornwall there were downfalls but nothing like the thousands of tons of water that hit Polperro.

Saturday, the next day, should have been one of the happiest days in the lives of Bridget Libby and Peter Bishop who were married at nearby Lansallos Church. They managed to smile for their wedding photographs, but the Vicar, the Reverend Edmund Allsopp, travelling from disaster-hit Polperro, encountered a landslide at Langreek forcing him to make a wide detour. But the Vicar did manage to get to the church on time! Lightning, however, had struck the church organ's electricity cable and fused it. Mr and Mrs Peter Bishop today run the Pottery Shop at Polperro.

Council workmen shovel sludge from the road outside the old forge.

Robert Hicks, the local MP recalls 'I visited the village on a number of occasions at the time of the serious floods in 1976, frequently with Vernon Seccombe, now Sir Vernon, who was then chairman of the Caradon District Council. A couple of years later the new harbour gate was installed. I recall making representations to the Minister at that time because under the existing provisions of the Polperro Harbour Order they were not allowed to borrow more than, I think, £100. I was responsible for making the appropriate representations to the Minister of Agriculture, Fisheries and Food for that figure to be increased so that it was more in line with modern day financial requirements.'

Following the flooding, South West Water and the National Rivers' Authority co-operated to install a flood warning siren at Saxon Bridge. The siren is activated by a rapid rise in the water level at the lower part of the village. Caradon District and Cornwall County Councils also regularly monitor the watercourse and remove any vegetation or debris that is obstructing the channel.

Mill Hill after the floodwaters subsided.

The Punch Bowl sign designed by the distinguished painter Augustus John.

Lanreath

THE delightful village of Lanreath, with its pretty cottages, manor house and Norman church, has an inn full of character – and history.

Back in the 1700s when Fowey was a busy, bustling port, full of sailing ships, coaches would have stopped at the Punch Bowl for refreshment –

refreshments for the driver and the passengers and, of course, the horses. In those days many of the local workers would have been employed in neighbouring industries and, before the days of mechanization, the farms would have needed scores, including women and children. The seventeenth century manor Court, on its own, would have required many for milking, harvesting and daily work around the farm and the land.

Bars at the Punch Bowl have always been known as kitchens – the Visitors' Kitchen once served as the courthouse. But the inn had its illicit side too – for it was a favourite haunt of the Polperro smugglers. Here they hid their cargo and from here they distributed it.

The inn sign at Lanreath is interesting in that forty years ago it was designed by the distinguished painter Augustus John. A friend of the landlord, he was a frequent visitor.

The author on a visit to Lanreath in the late 1960s was told an interesting story by Edna Oxley, then owner of both the inn and the old rectory. Her story linked church and inn:

'Long, long ago, Lanreath had a very old rector, who married a very young and very beautiful wife. The rector, though, was finding the parish a bit too much for him . . . there used to be about 2,000 in the parish . . . and he acquired the services of a young curate, a very charming young man. The inevitable happened. The curate and the rector's wife fell in love. Everybody in the village knew about the affair . . . that is, everybody except the rector. And, in his ignorance, the rector invited the curate to dinner one Christmas Day, but before the meal he suggested that the two of them should go down into the cellar to get a bottle of wine. Going down into the cellar the old man tripped and fell, and, as a result of the fall, died. Some of the villagers were suspicious about their rector's end, but they kept quiet. The funeral took place and the rector was laid to rest, and in time the curate became the rector and married the young widow.'

'But that wasn't the end of the old rector. He came back in the shape of a very black and very scurrilous cockerel and began haunting the rectory, tormenting the villagers, and young lovers in particular. He was a very wily cockerel, though, and nobody succeeded in catching him. Eventually, however, a group of local men, armed with pitch forks, cornered him in a barn, but again the cockerel was too wily for them. He flew over their heads and out of the barn, but he made the mistake of flying through an open window

An old photograph showing the inside of the Noughts and Crosses, a 16th century Polperro inn.

The strange accounting method used when the Noughts and Crosses was a bakehouse. The symbols represented amounts varying from half a penny to ten shillings – which was probably as high as an ordinary customer's credit was allowed to go.

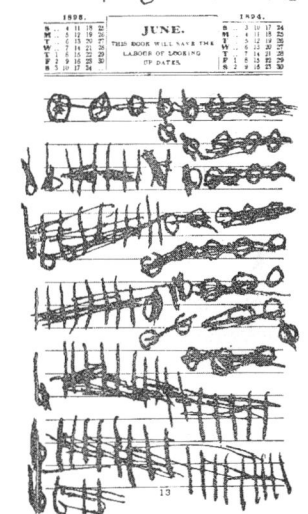

35

of the Punch Bowl. It so happened that the landlady was just taking bread out of her oven and the cockerel flew straight into the oven . . . and the landlady, with great presence of mind, slammed the door. That was the end of the cockerel and the old rector.

'The oven's still here today, still sealed off. Occasionally I've heard the cry of a cockerel, but it's usually turned out to be the cry of a real one somewhere outside . . .'

The Church of St Manarch and Dunstan at Lanreath has a great bell-ringing tradition. The Normans gave the village its first church and their stones are still in its nave and transept.

When Arthur Mee came here in the 1930s he wrote in his guide to Cornwall:

'The rarest treasures here are of wood. There are ancient carved timbers in all the roofs, a richly carved Elizabethan pulpit, a Jacobean font cover, and 17th century seats with poppyheads, among them people at prayer and a Saracen's head. There are modern pews given by a man who knew the church when he was young and remembered it in his prosperity; and an oak lectern in memory of Richard Buller, rector here for 53 years last century. The stocks are in the porch.'

The Giant's Hedge

ANY exploration of Polperro and district should include a visit to the Giant's Hedge.

Some say it's the Devil's best bit of architecture in the whole of the Westcountry. They recall a rhyme which runs:

'The Devil having nothing to do,

Built a great wall from Lerryn to Looe.'

It was the author and television personality Sally Jones who gave her publisher the precise directions. In her *Legends of Cornwall*, first published by Bossiney in 1980, Sally wrote: *'Surprisingly few people, even locals, knew of its existence when I investigated its whereabouts, and I drew a blank until the Lerryn farmer whose land it crosses gave me exact directions, including the great overhanging beech tree where a lane intersects it. Nowadays it is well-camouflaged by a thick covering of bracken, bushes and trees, so I felt*

The Giant's Hedge near Lerryn, photographed by Alice Boyd. An ancient king's boundary – or the work of the Devil?

a real thrill of discovery when I 'found' it for the first time, a wooded bank, eight yards wide and fifteen feet high in places, striding proudly alongside Ribby Wood, vanishing and then reappearing again, the broad, swathe clearly visible from most hilltops between Lerryn and Looe.'

The pure historians say our Satanic interpretation is all nonsense, pointing out it's just a fortification constructed in the sixth century by King Mark to keep out the attacking Irish. But we superstitious Cornish stand by the age-old belief: it's the work of the Devil.

Cornish ingenuity, when faced with a need to extend, produced this solution. It may look precarious but it has stood the test of time – and many customers.

Today's House of Props continues the tradition of providing tasty food for the visitor.

House of Props

THE HOUSE of Props is probably one of the most eccentric builings in all of Cornwall, in that it lives up to its name – its upstairs area is literally on props. One Polperro theory is that this curious arrangement was due to the extension being built over the river. One old picture postcard describes it as 'the most famous teahouse in England' – though Cornish Nationalists would say that Polperro is not in England!

Here are two illustrations separated by many years: our picture postcard comes from early in this century whereas Ray Bishop's photograph of the window and lunch menu was taken in 1991.

Lansallos

'HIGH above the sea stands its 15th century church, not far from Lantivet Bay, with a medieval tower embattled and pinnacled, and a porch (on which is a sundial of 1760) with a handsome roof giving us a clue to what lies within. It is the woodwork that is the chief treasure of the church.' That was Arthur Mee's impression on a visit in the 1930s.

Sir John Betjeman, coming here thirty years later, had this to say, *'The church (St Ildierna) looks unpromising outside . . . It has a charming light interior with granite arcades, old slate floors, old roofs and plastered walls and weathered and carved bench ends and remains of screen. With the cathedral glass removed it would be the pleasantest interior for miles.'*

Felicity Young's drawing, done early in 1992, shows that several of the headstones now lean all in the same direction – presumably all bent by the same winds.

The coast hereabouts is varied – the water often clear and deep and above the tiny beach of Lansallos Cove, a giant's view stretches westward from the hilltop right across St Austell Bay.

On page 40 an old photograph shows a secluded natural swimming place perhaps known only to the locals – the Chaypel Bathing Pool.

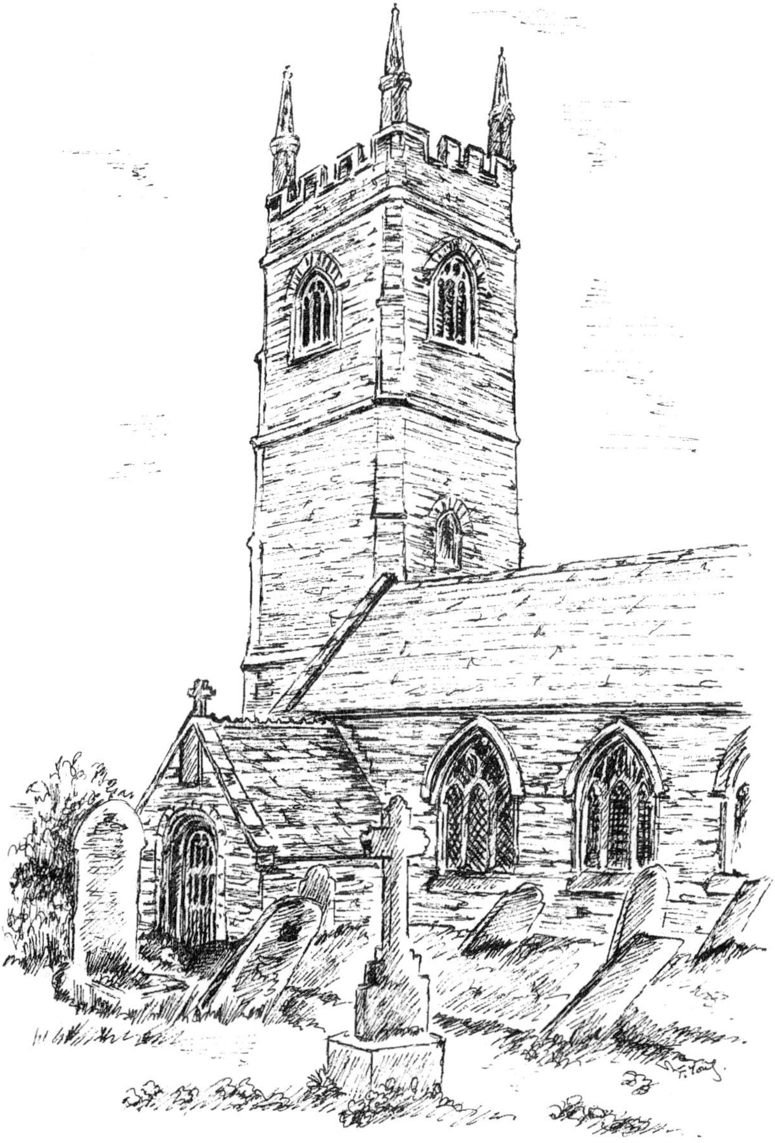

◀ *Lansallos Church*

Talland

TALLAND is another interesting location. Its ancient church has been the scene of some curious events. The vicar here in early Georgian times was one Richard Doidge. It is said *'He had such command over the spirit world that he could raise and lay ghosts at his will, and by a nod of his head banish them to the Red Sea. His parishioners looked up to him with great awe, and were afraid of meeting him at midnight, as he was sure then, whip in hand, to be pursuing and driving away the demons, that in all kinds of shapes were to be seen hovering around him. Amongst his other eccentricities he was fond of frequenting his churchyard at the dead of night!'*

And often Richard Doidge was not alone, for he had a good working relationship with the Polperro smugglers. The haunted reputation was such that the smugglers found it a very convenient place for storing their contraband. But those 'in the know' were sceptical about Doidge's powers of exorcism. They believed he used the story of apparitions in Bridles Lane, leading from Talland Beach, as a means of scaring off the excisemen. From spots like Talland and Lanreath the smuggled goods were shifted inland.

However, Doidge was not the only curious cleric of Talland. In the year 1812 the Reverend Whitmore, a curate here, absconded with the church's money. Proved an impostor and forger, he was eventually hanged on the gallows of Gloucester – and, as a result, some Cornish husbands and wives must have had dreadful doubts about the legality of their marriages!

But getting back to smuggling, Talland Churchyard is the resting place – an appropriate resting place – of one smuggler. Robert Mark was helmsman

Talland Church – on just one Sunday a year it throws open its doors to animal friends for a service to celebrate the birthday of the animal-loving St Francis of Assisi.

of the *The Three Friends*, a Polperro craft, which resisted capture by the revenue cutter. Robert Mark, in the wrong place at the wrong time, was killed by fire from the revenue cutter. His epitaph reads:

ROBERT MARK

late of Polperro, who Unfortunately
was shot at sea the 24th day of January
in the year of our Lord God 1802,
in the 40th Year of his Age

In prime of Life most suddenly,
Sad tidings to relate;
Here View My utter destiny,
and pity, My sad state:
I by a shot, which Rapid flew,
Was instantly struck dead;
Lord pardon the Offender who
My precious blood did shed.
Grant him to rest, and forgive Me,
All I have done amiss;
And that I may Rewarded be
With Everlasting Bliss.

The church of St John was built in 1838. Sir John Betjeman, who understood and loved his Cornish churches, said, on a visit here in the 1960s '... in the plain lancet style of Gothic ...'

A quiet harbour scene from a postcard sent shortly after the second world war. The sender describes Polperro as 'a very quaint little place – we prefer Looe ...' Not a sentiment echoed by many, if one can judge by the packed summer streets of Polperro today. Like other Cornish towns and villages it has had to come to terms with change. From being first mentioned as a fishing port in the 14th century, through an expansion which exploded into the prosperity of the pilchard fishing era, an end to smuggling, the decline of marine industries, and an acceptance that the holiday industry now reigns supreme – Polperro has kept its integrity, its unique charm and its quiet corners. Although old fish cellars have been converted into cafes and the boatman now trawls more for tourists to take round the waters than for fish, everywhere remnants of the old Polperro can be found if the visitor seeks them out. It may take more than one visit – but who is going to mind that?

MORE BOSSINEY BOOKS ...

EAST CORNWALL IN THE OLD DAYS
by Joy Wilson

GHOSTS OF CORNWALL
by Peter Underwood
Peter Underwood, President of the Ghost Club, journeys across haunted Cornwall. Photographs of haunted sites and drawings of ghostly characters all combine to prove that Cornwall is indeed a mystic land.

PARANORMAL IN THE WESTCOUNTRY
by Michael Williams

MYSTERIES IN THE CORNISH LANDSCAPE
by Tamsin Thomas

DISCOVERING BODMIN MOOR
by E.V. Thompson

LEGENDS OF CORNWALL
by Sally Jones

DAPHNE du MAURIER COUNTRY
by Martyn Shallcross
A special look at Cornwall in which the internationally-famous novelist set important stories.
'A treasure chest for those who love Cornwall and the du Maurier novels.'
Valerie Mitchell, The Packet Group of Newspapers

OLD PICTURE POSTCARDS OF CORNWALL
by Sara Paston-Williams

MORE BOSSINEY BOOKS ...

AROUND & ABOUT THE SMUGGLERS' WAYS
by David Mudd
Working through almost forty different sources, including the records of H.M. Customs & Excise itself, David Mudd (who discovered in the course of his research that his great-grandfather was a Customs officer) has produced a book that is as heady and addictive as the spirits, the wines and the tobaccos that once followed fish, tin and copper as Cornwall's great industries. Several of the sketches and many of the photographs are by David's wife, Diana.
'... *scrapes the romantic glitter from Cornwall's erstwhile illicit trade ... Meticulously researched and written in David Mudd's lively factual style it makes absorbing reading.*'

Alison Poole, Leader Group of Newspapers

THE CRUEL CORNISH SEA
by David Mudd
David Mudd selects more than 30 Cornish shipwrecks, spanning 400 years, in his fascinating account of seas and a coastline that each year claim their toll of human lives.
'*This is an important book.*'   Lord St Levan, The Cornish Times

We shall be pleased to send you our catalogue giving full details of our growing list of titles for Devon, Cornwall, Dorset and Somerset as well as forthcoming publications. If you have difficulty in obtaining our titles, write direct to Bossiney Books, Land's End, St Teath, Bodmin, Cornwall.